MIA & SEBASTIAN'S THEME

T0085415

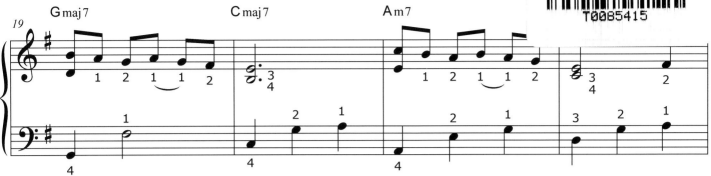

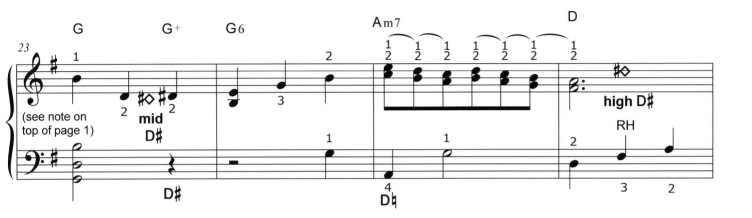

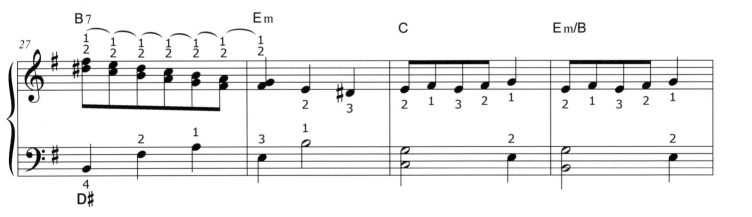

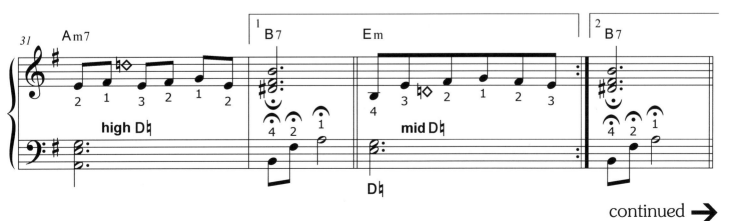

continued ➡

MIA & SEBASTIAN'S THEME

Slowly, very freely

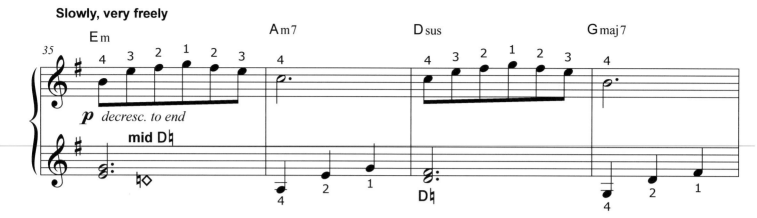

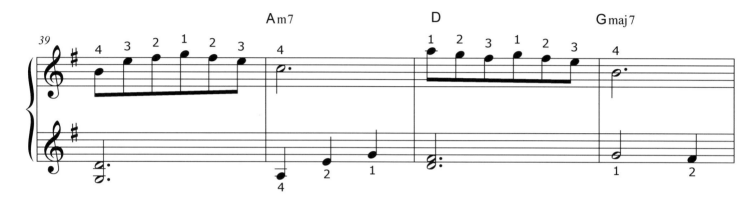

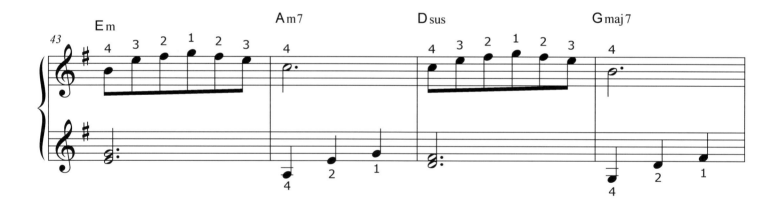

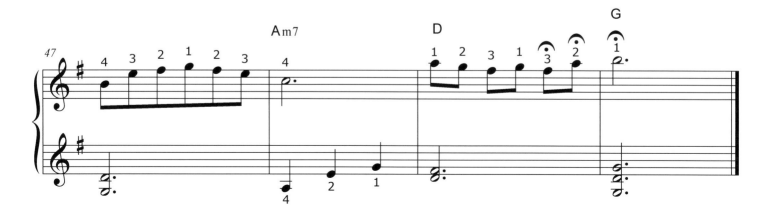

City of Stars
from LA LA LAND

Music by JUSTIN HURWITZ
Lyrics by BENJ PASEK & JUSTIN PAUL
Arranged for harp by SYLVIA WOODS

This piece should be played with a swing rhythm. The eighth notes are not played evenly, but "swung" like this:

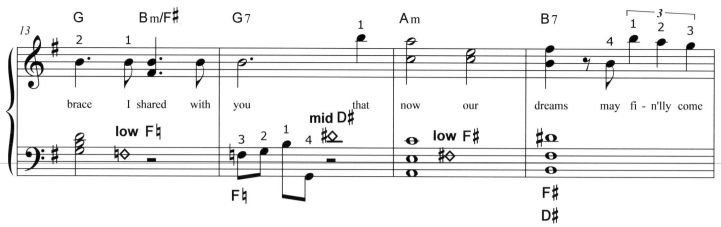

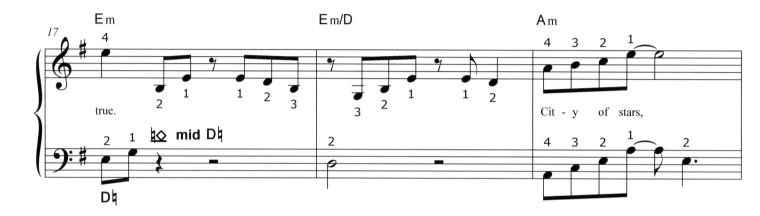

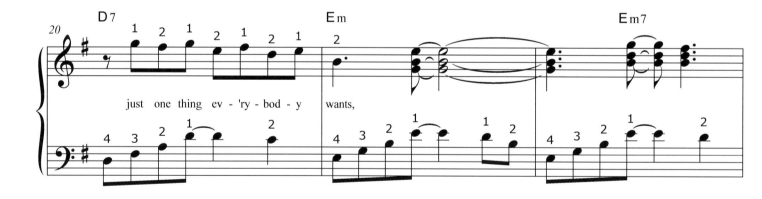

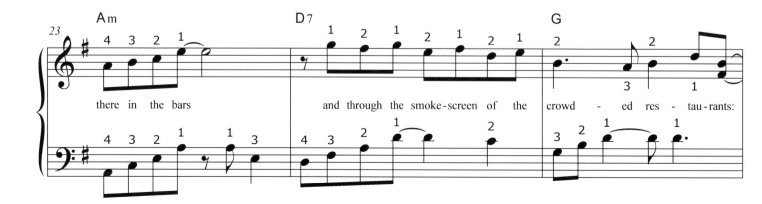

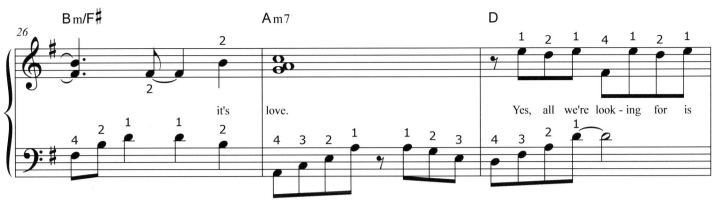

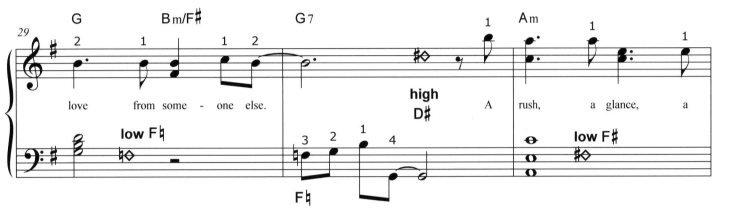

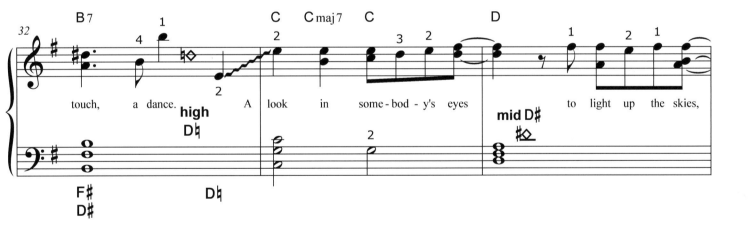

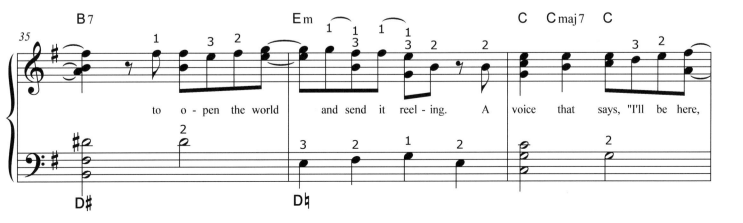

and you'll be al - right."

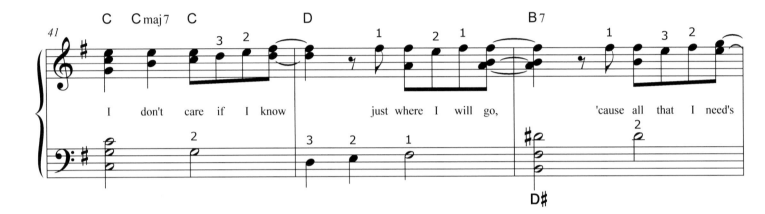

I don't care if I know   just where I will go,   'cause all that I need's

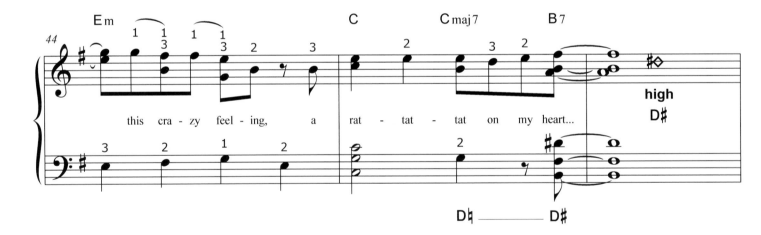

this cra - zy feel - ing, a   rat - tat - tat on my heart...

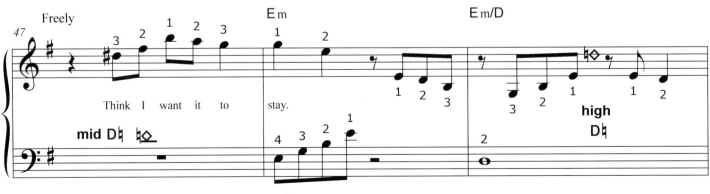

Think I want it to   stay.

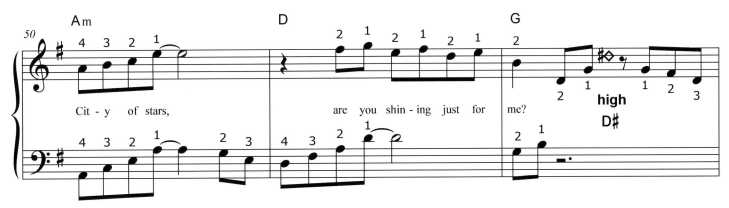

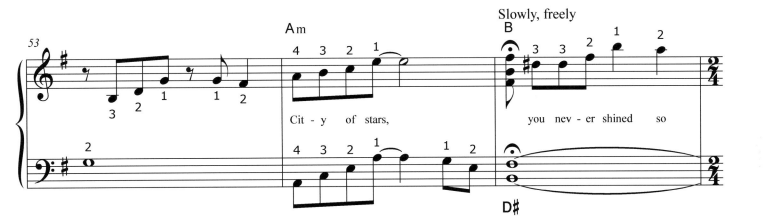

The Audition
(The Fools Who Dream)
from LA LA LAND

Music by JUSTIN HURWITZ
Lyrics by BENJ PASEK & JUSTIN PAUL
Arranged for harp by SYLVIA WOODS

All harp players: After you play the D-natural on beat 2 in measures 28 and 60, replace your 2nd finger on the D string to muffle it before you make the D-sharp lever or pedal change. This way, the string won't be ringing when you make the change.

Pedal harp players: Measures 12, 36, 44 and 86 require D-naturals and D-sharps on the same beat. Use the enharmonic E-flat for all D-sharps in the left hand in these measures, as indicated by the pedal changes printed below the bass clef.

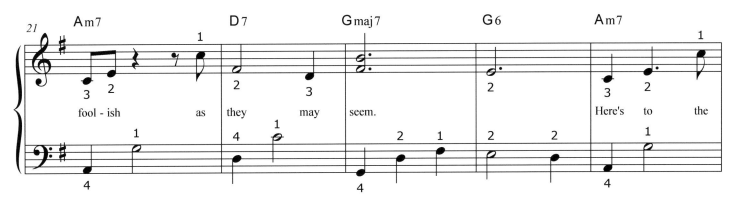

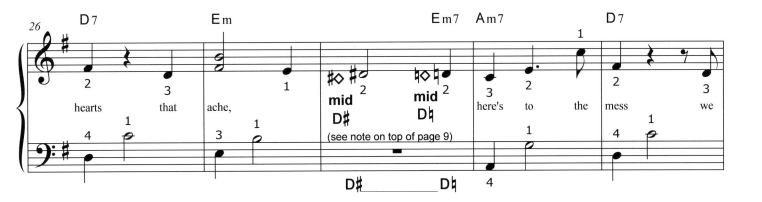

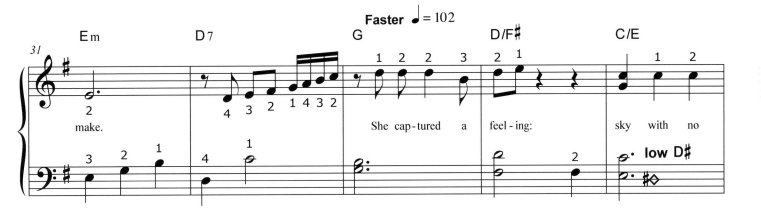

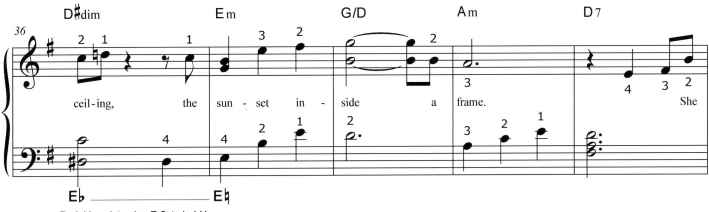

Pedal harpists play E-flats in LH.

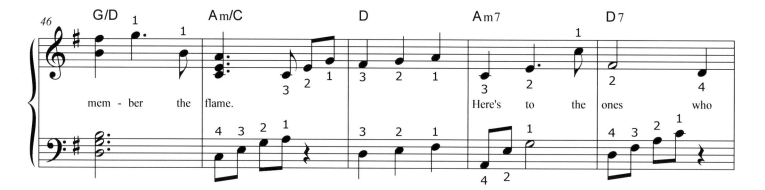

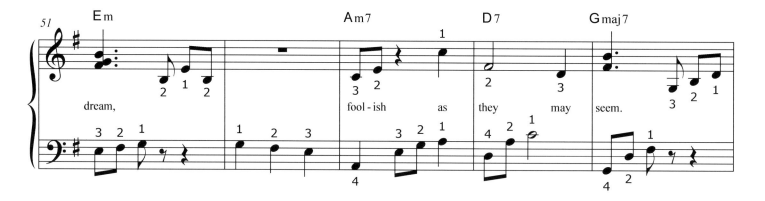

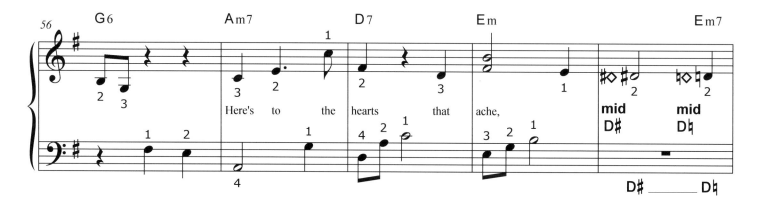

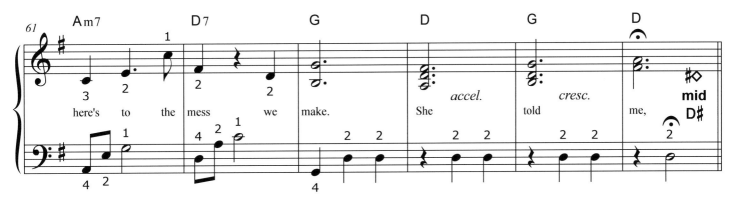

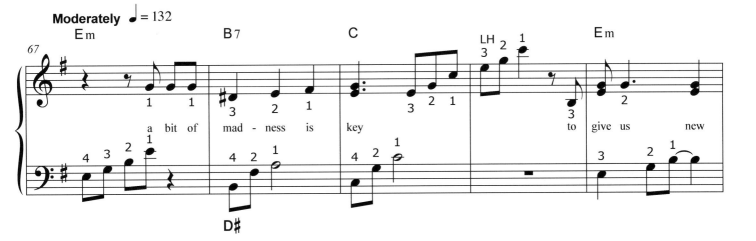

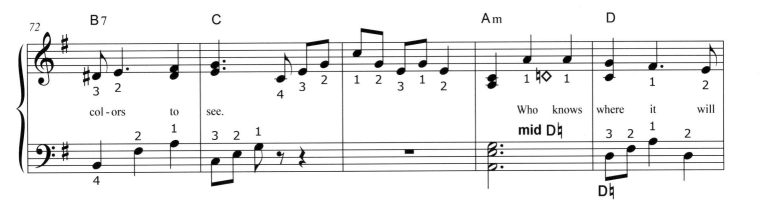

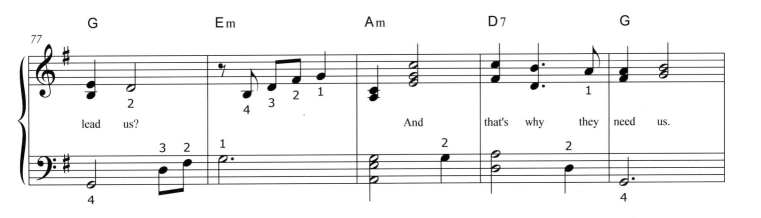

THE AUDITION

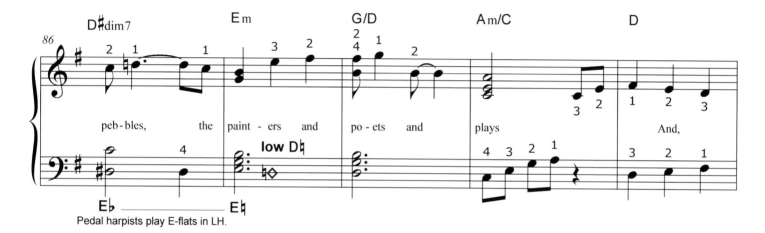

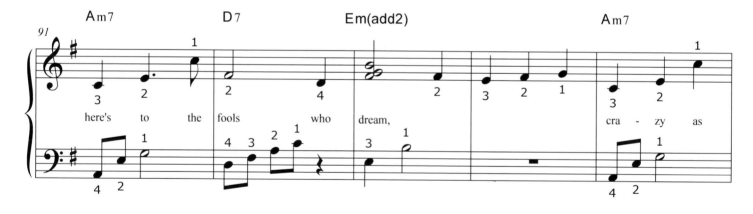

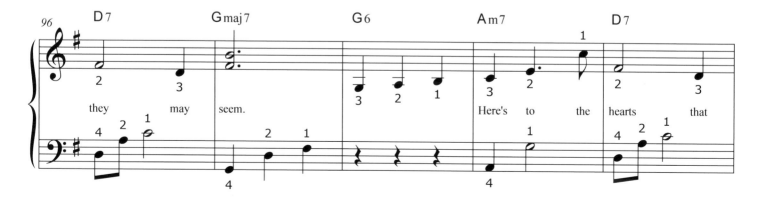